THE ULTIMATE MICROWAVABLE COOK BOOK FOR COLLEGE STUDENTS

HOME COOKED MEALS MADE IN UNDER 20 MINUTES!

My Husband Ta-Raj Benness is a very creative individual. Some people are artistic in so many ways drawing, painting, building. But Ta-Raj! His is in cooking cutting hair and fashion! People LOVE to eat and look good.

I am so proud of him and how he found his niche, it makes me smile when I see the out come. God as definitely blessed us/him when he found out what his passion is! Giving back and making people smile. This book will absolutely blow your mind when you see these creative recipes.

1st Peter 4:10 Each of you should use whatever gift you have received to serve others, as faithful stewards of God's grace in its various forms. (NIV)

---P.L. Benness

ALSO AVAILABLE "More Than a Conqueror the Life and Times of Ta-Raj Benness"

ISBN: 9798596060553

MICROWAVE RECIPES

"MACHO TACOS"

2 PACKS OF 6 OZ. FULLY COOKED READY-TO-EAT GROUND BEEF
1 PACK OF 3.6 OZ. FULLY COOKED CHUNK WHITE CHICKEN
(1) 5 OZ. HOT OR REGULAR BEEF FULLY COOKED SUMMER SAUSAGE
(1) 25 OZ. PK TACO SEASONING
(1) 7 OZ. RED CASERA SALSA
1/2 CUP JALAPENO WHEELS
(2) 4 OZ. STICKS OF MOZZARELLA CHEESE
(1) 6-PK FLOUR TORTILLAS

SLICE SUMMER SAUSAGE INTO SMALL CUBES.

PLACE IN LARGE MICROWAVABLE BOWL AND COOK FOR 60 SECONDS ON HIGH HEAT.

DRAIN OFF GREASE.

EMPTY GROUND BEEF AND CHICKEN PACK IN WITH SUMMER SAUSAGE ADDING 1/2 PACK OF TACO SEASONING.

MIX AND STIR. THEN COOK FOR 2 MIN. HIGH HEAT.

LET MEAT MIX REST.

CUT MOZZARELLA CHEESE UP IN SMALL SHREDDED PIECES AND PLACE IN SMALL SEPARATE CEREAL BOWL.

CUT JALAPENO WHEELS INTO SMALL PIECES PLACING INTO A SMALL BOWL.

MICROWAVE FOR 10 SECONDS.

PLACE ONE TORTILLA ON PAPER TOWEL AND MICROWAVE FOR 10 SECONDS.

FLIP IT OVER AND COOK FOR ANOTHER 10 SECONDS, THEN FOLD SHELL OVER ONCES.

SHELL SHOULD FOLD OVER EASILY BUT SHOULD HAVE A SLIGHTLY HARD CRUST TEXTURE.

HEAT FOR ADDITIONAL 10 SECONDS, IF NECESSARY.

TIME TO BUILD YOUR "MACHO TACOS"!!!

FILL COOKED TORTILLA HALF-WAY WITH MEAT MIXTURE.

TOP WITH SHREDDED MOZZARELLA, THEN TOP WITH JALAPENO WHEELS.

NEXT PLACE 2 HEAPING TEASPOONS OF RED CASERA SALSA ONTO TACO.

EAT AND ENJOY!!!!!

*OTHER SUGGESTED TOPPINGS: SOUR CREAM, OLIVES AND /OR SALSA VERDE.

TASTES GREAT AS A MEAL OR SERVE WITH NACHO CHEESE OR PLAIN CHIPS.

MAKES 6 TACOS.

"MACHO NACHOS" WITH HONEY GLAZE

(1) 4 OZ. SERVING OF NACHO CHEESE CHIPS
(1) 7 OZ. FULLY COOKED SHREDDED BEEF
(1) 3.6 OZ. FULLY COOKED CHUNK WHITE CHICKEN
(1) 5 OZ. FULLY COOKED SUMMER SAUSAGE HOT OR REGULAR
1/4 CUP OF INSTANT RICE
(1) 11 OZ. POUCH OF CHILI/ NO BEANS
1/2 CUP OF 'VELVEETA' SHARP SQUEEZE CHEESE
(1) 4 OZ. MOZZARELLA CHEESE STICK
1/4 CUP OF JALAPENO PEPPERS &/OR OLIVES
HONEY

DICE UP SUMMER SAUSAGE INTO SMALL CUBES.

PLACE IN A LARGE MICROWAVABLE BOWL AND COOK HIGH HEAT 1 MIN.

DRAIN GREASE.

ADD CHICKEN AND SHREDDED BEEF IN WITH SAUSAGE.

COOK FOR AN ADDITIONAL 3 MINS.

ADD RICE TO 1 CUP OF BOILING WATER AND COOK FOR 3 MINS. IN A SMALL BOWL.

COOK CHILI FOR 3 MIN. IN A SMALL BOWL.

COOK JALAPENO PEPPERS &/OR OLIVES IN A SMALL BOWL FOR 30 SECS.

DICE MOZZARELLA CHEESE, ADD SHARP CHEESE AND 1/4 CUP OF WATER.

COOK FOR 3 TO 4 MINS. UNTIL CHEESE HAS MELTED NICELY TOGETHER, LEAVING NO CHEESE CHUNKS.

OCCASIONALLY STIR TO AVOID SPILLAGE.

LET'S BUILD OUR "MACHO NACHOS"

PLACE NACHO CHIPS ON A PLATE OR IN A LARGE BOWL.

DRIZZLE HONEY OVER CHIPS LIGHTLY COATING THEM.

COOK FOR 1- 2 MINS. MOVING CHIPS AROUND OCCASIONALLY THROUGHOUT COOKING TIME. CAREFUL, DO NOT BURN.

POUR 1/2 OF CHEESE SAUCE OVER CHIPS.

ADD RICE, FOLLOWING WITH CHILI, MEAT MIXTURE, REST OF CHEESE SAUCE AND TOPPING IT OFF WITH JALAPENO PEPPERS &/OR OLIVES.

"LET'S DIG IN!!!!"

*SUGGESTED TOPPINGS: SOUR CREAM, SWEET AND HOT SAUCE, BBQ SAUCE, OR TACO SAUCE.

"GARLIC BREAD JUNK PIZZA"

2 PLAIN BAGELS
1/2 ROLL OF 'RITZ' CRACKERS
2 SINGLE FLOUR TORTILLA SHELLS
(2) 4 OZ. PASTA SAUCES
(1) 4 OZ. SWEET BBQ SAUCE
GARLIC POWDER
ITALIAN SEASONING
SUGAR
FRIED MINCED ONIONS
(1) 3.5 OZ. FULLY COOKED PKG OF PEPPERONI
(1) 3.6 OZ. FULLY COOKED CHUNK WHITE CHICKEN
(1) 6 OZ. FULLY COOKED GROUND BEEF
(1) 5 OZ. HOT OR REGULAR SUMMER SAUSAGE
(2) 4 OZ. MOZZARELLA CHEESE STICK
(1) 2.3 OZ. OLIVES
1/2 CUP JALAPENO WHEELS
1/2 CUP SHARP VELVEETA CHEESE

USE A SHEET OF MICROWAVABLE WAX PAPER OR USED PLASTIC CHIP BAG.

SLICE SUMMER SAUSAGE INTO SMALL CUBES, PLACING INTO LARGE MICROWAVABLE BOWL.

COOK FOR 60 SECONDS ON HIGH HEAT

DRAIN OFF GREASE.

EMPTY GROUND BEEF AND CHICKEN PACK IN WITH SUMMER SAUSAGE.

MIX AND STIR, THEN COOK FOR 2 MINS ON HIGH HEAT.

LET MEAT MIXTURE REST.

BREAK BAGELS AND TORTILLAS UP INTO SMALL PIECES PLACING INTO A LARGE MIXING BOWL.

CRUSH THE RITZ CRACKERS AND ALSO ADD INTO THE MIXING BOWL.

ADD 1 CUP OF WARM WATER INTO MIXTURE.

MIX TOGETHER WITH HANDS UNTIL THERE'S A DOUGH LIKE TEXTURE.

ADD A LITTLE WATER TO MIXTURE IF NECESSARY.

ADD 2 TABLESPOONS OF GARLIC POWDER AND 2 TABLESPOONS OF ITALIAN SEASONING.

MIX TOGETHER WITH HANDS AND PLACE ON WAX PAPER OR CUT OPEN PLASTIC CHIP BAG.

BEGIN FORMING YOUR PIE CRUST INTO A CIRCULAR SHAPE. CRUST SHOULDN'T BE ANY THICKER THEN 1/2 INCH.

NEXT PLACE CRUST INTO THE MICROWAVE FOR 90 SEC. THEN ROTATE AND COOK FOR AN ADDITIONAL 60 SEC.

REMOVE CRUST FROM MICROWAVE AND LET REST. CRUST SHOULD BE COOKED HAVING A SOFT DRY TEXTURE.

NEXT MIX PASTA SAUCE AND BBQ SAUCE INTO A SMALL CEREAL BOWL.

ADD 2 TEASPOONS OF SUGAR AND 1 TEASPOON OF ITALIAN SEASONING TO THE SAUCE.

MIX TOGETHER.

TIME TO BUILD YOUR "GARLIC BREAD JUNK PIZZA"

WITH A SPOON, POUR AND SMOOTH OUT PIZZA SAUCE ONTO CRUST AND DISTRIBUTE EVENLY.

ADD MEAT MIXTURE ON TOP OF SAUCE. DISTRIBUTE EVENLY.

ADD PEPPERONI. DISTRIBUTE EVENLY

ADD 1/2 CUP OF MINCED ONIONS AND 2 TABLESPOONS OF BUTTER IN A SMALL CEREAL BOWL.

HEAT IN MICROWAVE FOR 10 SECS. OPEN AND STIR, THEN REPEAT.

LOOK FOR ONIONS TO BE A LIGHT GOLDEN BROWN. DO NOT BURN.

CUT MOZZARELLA CHEESE INTO SMALL SHREDDED PIECES.

PLACE IN A MICROWAVABLE BOWL AND ADD 1/2 CUP OF WATER OR MILK.

COOK ON HIGH HEAT FOR 2 MINS.

OPEN STIR AND ADD IN SHARP VELVEETA. REPEAT UNTIL CHEESE IS MELTED. LEAVING NO CHUNKS OF CHEESE IN THE BOWL.

ONCE CHEESE IS MELTED AND CREAMY, ADD ONIONS.

STIR TOGETHER AND POUR ON TO THE PIZZA. DISTRIBUTE EVENLY.

TAKE A PINCH OF ITALIAN SEASONING AND LIGHTLY DUST THE TOP OF THE PIZZA.

READY TO EAT??????

ADD GRATED ITALIAN CHEESE FOR GARNISH.

MAKES 1 LARGE PIZZA.

CROQUETTES

(2) 6 OZ. FULLY COOKED FILLET OF MACKEREL (IN OIL)
(1) 3.6 OZ FULLY COOKED CHUNK WHITE CHICKEN
1/2 ROLL OF 'RITZ' UNSALTED CRACKERS
1/2 CUP JALAPENO WHEELS
BLACK PEPPER
LAWRY'S SEASONING SALT
UNSALTED BUTTER

EMPTY MACKEREL AND CHICKEN PK INTO A LARGE MIXING BOWL.

CRUSH 1/2 PKG OF 'RITZ' CRACKERS INTO BOWL WITH MEAT.

DICE JALAPENO WHEELS INTO SMALL CUBES AND ADD TO MIXTURE.

ADD 1/2 TEASPOON OF LAWRY'S SEASONING SALT.

MIX TOGETHER USING HANDS.

BEGIN FORMING APPROXIMATELY 8 SMALL PATTIES.

USING A LONG MICROWAVABLE CONTAINER, ADD 2 TEASPOONS OF BUTTER INTO CONTAINER.

PLACE IN MICROWAVE FOR 10 SECONDS.

ONCE BUTTER HAS MELTED PLACE PATTIES INTO THE CONTAINER, LEAVING A SMALL GAP IN BETWEEN EACH CROQUETTE.

NEXT DUST BLACK PEPPER ALONG TOP OF CROQUETTES.

COOK FOR 10 MINS. ON HIGH HEAT.

LOOK FOR A LIGHT GOLDEN-BROWN COLOR TO FORM. DO NOT OVER COOK.

LET THEM REST FOR 10 MINS. AT LEAST.

READY TO ENJOY!!!!

MAKES 2 SERVINGS.

TASTES GREAT AS A MEAL. BUT CAN ENJOY WITH RICE, NOODLES, OR BREAD.

*SUGGESTED SAUCES: HOT SAUCE OR TARTAR SAUCE

FRIED "CATFISH" FILLETS &/OR NUGGETS

(1) 6 OZ. FILLET OF MACKEREL (IN OIL)
2 ROLLS OF 'RITZ' UNSALTED CRACKERS
HONEY
LAWRY'S SEASONING SALT
BLACK PEPPER
UNSALTED BUTTER

EMPTY MICROWAVE POPCORN BAG.

PLACE MACKEREL IN A LARGE MICROWAVEABLE BOWL.

TAKE BOTH ROLLS OF CRACKERS AND CRUSH THEM, WHILE LEAVING THEM IN THE PLASTIC.

EMPTY 1/2 A ROLL IN THE BOWL WITH MACKEREL.

MIX TOGETHER USING HANDS UNTIL YOU NO LONGER SEE ANY CRACKERS.

NEXT BEGIN TO FORM YOUR FILLETS OR NUGGETS.

FILLETS SHOULD BE 1/2 INCH THICK AND HAVE A FOOTBALL SHAPE TO THEM (OVAL).

WITH REMAINING CRACKERS, CRUSH UNTIL THEY BECOME LIKE FINE DUST. HAVING NO CHUNKS.

PLACE IN A LARGE SEPARATE BOWL, ADDING 1/2 TEASPOON OF LAWRY'S SEASONING SALT AND 1 TABLESPOON OF BLACK PEPPER.

MIX TOGETHER.

TAKE HONEY AND EVENLY COAT BOTH SIDES OF THE FILLETS OR NUGGETS.

IMMEDIATELY ROLL THE FILLET OR NUGGET IN THE SEASONED CRACKER MIXTURE.

PLACE THEM TO THE SIDE AND REPEAT UNTIL ALL THE FISH IS COATED IN THE CRACKER MIXTURE.

RIP OPEN YOUR POPCORN BAG AND LAY FLAT WITH THE INSIDE OF THE BAG FACING IN AN UPWARD POSITION.

LIGHTLY COAT THE SURFACE OF THE BAG WITH BUTTER, THEN LAY THE FILLETS OR NUGGETS ON THE BAG.

COOK THE FILLETS ON HIGH HEAT FOR 6 MINS. LOOK FOR GOLDEN BROWN COLOR, WITH SOME FIRMNESS TO THEM. DO NOT OVER COOK.

COOK THE NUGGETS ON HIGH HEAT FOR 3 MINS.

NOTE: MAY NEED TO COOK FOR ADDITIONAL MINUTES IF FISH IS TOO SOFT.

ONCE OUT OF THE MICROWAVE, LET REST FOR 5 MINS. AND LIGHTLY DUST FILLETS OR NUGGETS WITH LAWRY'S SEASONING SALT AGAIN.

TIME TO EAT FOLKS!!!!!!

MAKES UP TO 2 BIG FILLETS OR 6 NUGGETS.

TASTES GREAT AS A MEAL, BUT GOES WELL WITH MAC AND CHEESE, SPAGHETTI, OR FRIED RICE.

*SUGGESTED SAUCES: HONEY MUSTARD, SWEET & HOT, RANCH, HOT SAUCE, OR BBQ SAUCE

"GRANDMA'S FAMOUS CHICKEN AND DUMPLINGS"

(2) 6 OZ. FULLY COOKED CHUNK WHITE CHICKEN
1 CUP OF DICED CARROTS
1 CUP OF DICED CELERY
1 RAMEN NOODLE CREAMY CHICKEN SEASONING
MILK
PEPPER
GARLIC POWDER
SALT
1.5 PLAIN BAGEL
(1) 4 OZ. MOZZARELLA CHEESE STICK

BOIL CARROTS AND CELERY IN 5 CUPS OF WATER FOR 15-20 MINS., USING A LARGE MICROWAVABLE BOWL.

ADD CREAMY CHICKEN SEASONING ONCE WATER BEGINS TO BOIL.
THEN STIR.

ADD CHICKEN AND COOK FOR AN ADDITIONAL 5 MINS.

REMOVE BOWL FROM MICROWAVE.

CUT MOZZARELLA CHEESE INTO SMALL CUBES.

PLACE IN A MICROWAVABLE BOWL AND ADD 1/2 CUP OF MILK.

COOK CHEESE UNTIL IT BECOMES NICE AND CREAMY.

FREQUENTLY STOP AND STIR TO PREVENT SPILLAGE.

ADD CHEESE AND STIR WITH CHICKEN AND VEGGIES.

DUMPLINGS:

BREAK BAGELS INTO SMALL PIECES.

PLACE IN A BOWL AND WET PIECES WITH 1/2 CUP OF WATER.

MIX WITH HANDS AND FLATTEN OUT DOUGH ON A FLAT SURFACE (WAX PAPER PREFERABLY) MAKING IT 1/4 INCH THICK.

COOK DOUGH FOR 2 MINS., THEN ROTATE AND COOK FOR ANOTHER MIN. DOUGH SHOULD BE DRY AND SOFT.

NEXT REMOVE DOUGH FROM MICROWAVE AND PROCEED TO CUT OUT SMALL SQUARE SHAPED DUMPLINGS.

ADD TO CHICKEN AND VEGGIES.

ADD 1/2 TEASPOON OF SALT, 1 TEASPOON OF PEPPER AND 1 TEASPOON OF GARLIC.

COOK FOR 5 MINS. STIR AND SERVE.

SERVING SIZE: 2

EGG ROLLS WITH PEANUT BUTTER DIPPING SAUCE

(1) 6 PK FLOUR TORTILLA SHELLS
(1) 3.6 OZ. FULLY COOKED CHUNK WHITE CHICKEN
(1) 5 OZ. FULLY COOKED HOT OR REGULAR SUMMER SAUSAGE
(1) 6 OZ. FILLET OF MACKEREL (IN OIL)
1- 'THAI PALACE' THAI RICE NOODLE
1/2 CUP OF CHUNKY PEANUT BUTTER
1 CUP OF SWEET AND HOT SAUCE
1/4 CUP OF SRIRACHA HOT CHILI SAUCE
1 CUP OF VEGETABLES FLAKES

EGG ROLLS:

DICE SUMMER SAUSAGE INTO SMALL THIN STRIPS.

PLACE INTO A LARGE MICROWAVABLE BOWL.

COOK IN MICROWAVE HIGH HEAT FOR 90 SEC. DRAIN OFF GREASE.

PLACE CHICKEN IN WITH SAUSAGE.

DRAIN OIL FROM MACKEREL AND ADD IT IN WITH SAUSAGE & CHICKEN, SHREDDING APART BOTH MEATS WITH A FOLK.

COOK ON HIGH HEAT FOR 2 MINS. KEEP COVERED WITH LID TO AVOID MACKEREL FROM POPPING OUT DUE TO HIGH HEAT.

ONCE DONE, LET MEAT REST.

BREAK THAI NOODLE IN HALF, THEN OPEN PACKAGE AND REMOVE THE SEASONING, OIL PK, AND VEGETABLE PK.

ADD NOODLES TO A BOWL OF HOT WATER.

COOK FOR 2 MINS.

DRAIN, THEN RINSE OFF WITH COLD WATER, & DRAIN AGAIN. LET NOODLES SIT.

COOK VEGETABLE FLAKES IN A SMALL CUP WITH A SMALL AMOUNT OF HOT WATER. COOK FOR 2 MINS.

DRAIN WATER.

REMOVE 1 TORTILLA FROM PKG, WET HAND WITH WATER, & GENTLY RUB BOTH SIDES OF THE TORTILLA, FULLY WETTING & COATING BOTH SIDES. CAREFUL NOT TO APPLY TO MUCH.

PLACE TORTILLA ONTO BOWL LID AND COOK ON HIGH HEAT FOR 10 SECS.

FLIP OVER AND COOK FOR ADDITIONAL 10 SECS.

TIME TO ASSEMBLE YOUR EGG ROLLS!

PULL A SMALL AMOUNT OF THAI NOODLE FROM BOWL AND PLACE IN THE CENTER OF THE TORTILLA.

ADD 2 TABLESPOONS OF MEAT MIXTURE ON TOP OF NOODLES.

ADD 1 TABLESPOON OF VEGETABLE FLAKES ON TOP OF MEAT.

FOLD THE SIDES OF THE TORTILLA THE SHORT WAY, THEN PROCEED TO TIGHTLY ROLL THE TORTILLA THE OPPOSITE WAY. ALL WHILE TUCKING THE FILLING INSIDE THE TORTILLA.

RIGHT BEFORE COMPLETELY CLOSING THE TORTILLA, ADD A SMALL AMOUNT OF WATER TO YOUR FINGER TIPS AND LIGHTLY APPLY TO THE EDGE OF THE TORTILLA CREATING A SEALER.

HEAT FOR 10 SECS. AND LET REST. REPEAT TO FINISH THE OTHER EGG ROLLS.

PEANUT BUTTER DIPPING SAUCE:

ADD PEANUT BUTTER, SRIRACHA SAUCE, AND SWEET AND HOT IN WITH 1/2 CUP OF HOT WATER. STIR AND HEAT FOR 2 MIN.

EAT AND ENJOY!

SERVING SIZE: 2

LASAGNA 4 MEAT 4 CHEESE

(6) PKGS. RAMEN NOODLE (ANY KIND)
(1) 3.5 OZ. FULLY COOKED PEPPERONI
(1) 3.6 OZ. FULLY COOKED CHUNK WHITE CHICKEN
(1) 6 OZ. FULLY COOKED GROUND BEEF
(1) 5 OZ. FULLY COOKED SUMMER SAUSAGE HOT OR REGULAR
1 CUP OF 'VELVEETA' JALAPENO SQUEEZE CHEESE
(1) 2 OZ. PKG OF CREAM CHEESE
1/2 CUP OF 'VELVEETA SHARP SQUEEZE CHEESE
(1) 4 OZ. MOZZARELLA CHEESE STICK
(2) 4 OZ. PASTA SAUCE
1/2 CUP OF SWEET BBQ SAUCE
1 TEASPOON OF SUGAR
ITALIAN SEASONING

DICE SUMMER SAUSAGE INTO SMALL CUBES.

COOK ON HIGH HEAT FOR 2 MIN. DRAIN GREASE.

ADD CHICKEN IN WITH SAUSAGE, ALSO ADD IN GROUND BEEF. COOK FOR 3 MIN.

COOK PEPPERONI FOR 1 MIN. IN ITS PACKAGE, THEN LET IT REST.

MIX PASTA SAUCE, SUGAR, AND BBQ SAUCE TOGETHER IN A SMALL BOWL. COOK FOR 1 MIN.

PLACE RAMEN NOODLES IN A LARGE LONG MICROWAVABLE CONTAINER. DO NOT BREAK UP NOODLES, LEAVE WHOLE.

POUR BOILING HOT WATER OVER NOODLES, EMERGING THEM ALL UNDER WATER. LEAVE FOR 2 MIN. AND THEN DRAIN.

DISCARD SEASONING PKG.

DON'T OVER COOK, AS SOON AS NOODLES HAVE A LITTLE SOFTNESS TO THEM, QUICKLY DRAIN OFF WATER. TRY TO KEEP EACH NOODLE IN IT'S ORIGINAL FORM.

REMOVE 3 PKG OF NOODLES LEAVING THE REMAINING 3 IN THE CONTAINER.

SPREAD OUT THE LONG WAY AND LAY EACH PKG OF NOODLES FLAT IN THE CONTAINER, COVERING THE ENTIRE BOTTOM OF CONTAINER.

MIX JALAPENO CHEESE, CREAM CHEESE, AND SHARP CHEESE TOGETHER WITH 1/4 CUP OF WATER.

COOK FOR 2 MIN. STIR UNTIL CHEESE IS MELTED AND CREAMY.

POUR 1/2 OF THE MELTED CHEESE OVER THE NOODLES THAT'S IN THE CONTAINER. DISTRIBUTE EVENLY.

POUR HALF OF THE BOWL OF SAUCE OVER THE CHEESE. DISTRIBUTE EVENLY.

POUR THE COOKED MEAT IN, DISTRIBUTE EVENLY, TOPPING THE MEAT WITH PEPPERONI.

TOP WITH THE REMAINING 3 PKGS, OF NOODLES, STRETCHING AND LAYING THEM OUT COMPLETELY COVERING THE MEAT.

POUR THE REST OF THE SAUCE OVER NOODLES.

POUR THE REST OF THE CHEESE OVER THE SAUCE AND DISTRIBUTE EVENLY.

COOK LASAGNA ON HIGH HEAT FOR 5 MIN. THEN REMOVE FROM MICROWAVE.

IN A SMALL BOWL MELT MOZZARELLA, USING 1/4 CUP OF WATER.

ONCE MELTED AND CREAMY WITHOUT CHUNKS, POUR EVENLY OVER LASAGNA AND DUST WITH ITALIAN SEASONING.

COOK FOR ANOTHER 4 MINS.

LET REST FOR 20 MIN THEN CUT 8 EVEN DECENT SIZE SQUARES.

"DINNERS READY"

SERVING SIZE: 4

SPAGHETTI BAKE

(1) 16 OZ. PK. OF ANGEL HAIR PASTA
(1) 7 OZ. FULLY COOKED SHREDDED BEEF
(1) 5 OZ. FULLY COOKED SUMMER SAUSAGE HOT OR REGULAR
(1) 6 OZ. FULLY COOKED GROUND BEEF
(4) 4 OZ. PASTA SAUCES
1 CUP OF SWEET BBQ SAUCE
1/2 CUP OF DICED BELL PEPPER &/ OR JALAPENO
1/4 CUP OF DICED ONIONS
1 CUP OF 'VELVEETA' SHARP SQUEEZE CHEESE
(2) 4 OZ. MOZZARELLA CHEESE STICK
(2) 2 OZ. CREAM CHEESE

FILL LARGE MICROWAVEABLE BOWL WITH WATER, ADD A PINCH OF SALT, AND BRING WATER TO A BOIL.

POUR IN ANGEL HAIR AND COOK FOR 3-5 MIN.

DRAIN WATER, RINSE WITH COLD WATER, REPEAT.

USE A LARGE MICROWAVABLE BOWL TO COOK MEAT.

DICE SUMMER SAUSAGE INTO SMALL CUBES, COOK ON HIGH HEAT FOR 1 MIN. DRAIN GREASE.

ADD IN SHREDDED BEEF, AND GROUND BEEF WITH SUMMER SAUSAGE.

COOK HIGH HEAT FOR 3 MIN.

MIX PASTA SAUCE AND BBQ SAUCE TOGETHER IN A MICROWAVABLE BOWL.

SAUTE ONIONS, BELL PEPPERS, &/OR JALAPENOS IN 2 TABLESPOONS OF BUTTER FOR 3 MINS.

ADD TO SAUCE AND COOK SAUCE FOR 5 MIN. ON HIGH HEAT.

ADD ALL 3 CHEESES TO A MICROWAVEABLE BOWL WITH 1/2 CUP OF WATER.

COOK UNTIL CHEESE IS MELTED AND CREAMY, HAVING NO CHUNKS OF CHEESE LEFT. OCCASIONALLY STOP AND STIR, TO PREVENT SPILLAGE.

NEXT SPLIT PASTA IN HALF SEPARATING AND USING ANOTHER BOWL.

ADD 1/2 BOWL OF PASTA SAUCE, AND 1/2 BOWL OF MEAT MIXTURE TO 1/2 BOWL OF PASTA.
MIX TOGETHER.

TOP WITH MELTED CHEESE AND SPREAD OUT EVENLY. REPEAT.

ADD THE OTHER HALF OF PASTA SAUCE, MEAT MIXTURE, AND PASTA.
THEN TOP WITH REMAINING CHEESE.

COOK SPAGHETTI BAKE FOR 10 MINS. ON HIGH HEAT.

WHEN DONE, DUST WITH ITALIAN SEASONING. LET REST FOR 20 MIN.

DINNER IS SERVED!!!!!!!!

SERVING SIZE: 5

ITALIAN BEEF ROLLS &/OR BAGEL SANDWICH WITH CHEESE

(2) 7 OZ. FULLY COOKED SHREDDED BEEF
1 MIXED CUP OF DICED JALAPENO, GREEN, RED, YELLOW, PEPPERS
1 RAMEN NOODLE BEEF SEASONING
1 TABLESPOON OF GARLIC POWDER
1 TABLESPOON OF SUGAR
(1) 6 PKG. OF FLOUR TORTILLA SHELLS (2 PLAIN BAGELS FOR SANDWICHES)
(2) 4 OZ. MOZZARELLA CHEESE STICK
1/4 CUP OF ITALIAN SEASONING
1/4 UNSALTED BUTTER
1 CALIFORNIA VEGETABLE RAMEN CUP OF SOUP

PLACE SHREDDED BEEF IN A LARGE MICROWAVABLE BOWL. COOK HIGH HEAT FOR 6 MIN.

DICE PEPPERS IN VERY SMALL PIECES, PLACE IN A SEPARATE MICROWAVEABLE BOWL, ADD BUTTER, AND SAUTE FOR 10 MINS.

ADD TO SHREDDED BEEF.

BOIL CUP OF SOUP. WHEN DONE DRAIN WATER IN WITH SHREDDED BEEF AND PEPPERS. DISCARD NOODLES.

NEXT ADD SUGAR, GARLIC, BEEF, AND ITALIAN SEASONING. STIR IN AND COOK ON HIGH HEAT FOR 5 MINS.
BEGIN MELTING CHEESE IN A LARGE MICROWAVABLE BOWL WITH 1/4 CUP OF WATER.

MELT CHEESE UNTIL CREAMY AND NO CHUNKS OF CHEESE ARE REMAINING.

USING A MICROWAVABLE BOWL LID, TAKE 1 TORTILLA, WET YOUR HANDS WITH WARM WATER. WET BOTH SIDES OF TORTILLA. PLACE TORTILLA ON THE LID AND COOK FOR 10 SEC. THEN FLIP OVER AND REPEAT ON THE OTHER SIDE.

APPLY 2 TABLESPOONS OF MELTED CHEESE DOWN THE MIDDLE OF THE TORTILLA.

ADD 3 HEAPING TABLESPOONS OF DRAINED BEEF DOWN THE MIDDLE OF THE TORTILLA AS WELL.

FOLD IN SIDES OF THE TORTILLA, ROTATE, TUCK AND ROLL IN TIGHTLY THE OTHER SIDES.

BEFORE COMPLETING THE ROLL, WET FINGERTIPS WITH WATER AND LIGHTLY TAP THE EDGE OF THE TORTILLA, SEALING THE ROLL.

HEAT ROLL FOR 10 SECS. AND REPEAT UNTIL ALL ROLLS ARE ASSEMBLED.

FOR BAGEL SANDWICHES, WARM BAGELS FOR 5 SECS.

SPLIT BEEF MIXTURE IN HALF AND BUILD EACH SANDWICH.

FOR ITALIAN BEEF ROLLS SLICE DOWN THE MIDDLE & CUT IN HALF.

PLACE IN BOWL WITH PAPER TOWEL UNDERNEATH IN UPWARD POSITION.

APPLY CHEESE EVENLY TO BOTH SANDWICHES.

ENJOY YOUR ITALIAN BEEFS!!!!

TASTE GREAT AS A MEAL, COULD SERVE WITH CHILI CHEESE FRIES, OR POTATO CHIPS.

SERVING SIZE: 2

HOMEMADE MEAT LOAF

(5) 6 OZ. FULLY COOKED GROUND BEEF
1 ROLL OF 'RITZ' CRACKERS
1/2 ROLL OF 'SALTINE' UNSALTED CRACKERS
1/2 CUP OF INSTANT POWDER EGGS
1 CUP OF DICED ONIONS, BELL PEPPERS, &/OR JALAPENO PEPPERS
1/2 CUP OF SWEET BBQ SAUCE OR KETCHUP

ADD GROUND BEEF TO A LARGE MIXING BOWL.

CRUSH ROLLS OF CRACKERS AND ADD TO GROUND BEEF.

FOLLOW WITH DICED VEGGIES.

ADD EGGS TO 1 CUP OF WATER, BEAT AND POUR INTO MEAT LOAF.

MIX TOGETHER WITH HANDS THOROUGHLY.

USING A MEDIUM, NARROW SIZE MICROWAVABLE BOWL, PLACE MEAT INTO IT.

PACK DOWN AND LET SET FOR A FEW HOURS. COOK FOR 10 TO 15 MINS.

CHECK ON IT THROUGHOUT COOKING TIME, ROTATING AND CHECKING FOR FIRMNESS AND A GOLDEN-BROWN LOOK. CAREFUL NOT TO BURN.

DURING THE LAST 2 MIN. OF COOKING TIME, APPLY BBQ SAUCE OR KETCHUP ACROSS THE TOP.

COOK FOR AN ADDITIONAL 2 MINS.

LET REST FOR AT LEAST 1 HOUR.

CUT IN THICK SLICES.

"MMMMMBOYEEEE, LETS EAT!!!!"

*SUGGESTED SERVING SIDES: MASH POTATOES & GRAVY, MAC & CHEESE, &/OR CORN.

SERVING SIZE:5

CHICKEN TENDERS

(2) 3.6 OZ. FULLY COOKED CHUNK WHITE CHICKEN
1 ROLL OF 'RITZ' UNSALTED CRACKERS
HONEY
UNSALTED BUTTER
USED MICROWAVABLE POPCORN BAG
1/2 TABLESPOON LAWRY'S SEASONING SALT
1 TABLESPOON BLACK PEPPER

PLACE CHICKEN INTO A LARGE MICROWAVABLE BOWL.

CRUSH 1/4 CRACKERS INTO A FINE DUST & APPLY TO CHICKEN.

PLACE REMAINING CRACKERS INTO A SEPARATE BOWL.

ADD LAWRY'S & PEPPER & MIX TOGETHER.

MIX CHICKEN & CRACKERS TOGETHER USING HANDS, THEN BEGIN TO FORM THE TENDERS.
(SHOULD MAKE 4-5 TENDERS)

NEXT DRIZZLE HONEY ONTO TENDERS, FULLY COATING BOTH SIDES.

ROLL EACH ONE IN THE CRACKERS, COATING EACH SIDE.

WITH POPCORN BAG, CUT OPEN & MAKE SURE THAT THE INSIDE IS FACING UPWARDS.

SPREAD A THIN LAYER OF BUTTER ON THE INSIDE OF BAG.

PLACE CHICKEN ON BAG AND COOK ON HIGH HEAT FOR 2 TO 3 MINS.

FLIP TENDERS & REPEAT.

DO NOT OVER-COOK. LOOK FOR GOLDEN BROWN COLOR.

"JUST IN TIME. LET'S EAT"

*SUGGESTED SAUCE: HONEY MUSTARD, BBQ, SWEET & HOT, OR HOT SAUCE.

SERVING SIZE: 1

QUESADILLAS (MEAT LOVERS)

(1) 6 PKG. OF FLOUR TORTILLA SHELLS
1 MOZZARELLA CHEESE STICK
(2) 2 OZ. CREAM CHEESE W/JALAPENO
1/2 CUP 'VELVEETA' SHARP CHEESE
(2) 4 OZ. PASTA SAUCE
(2) 6 OZ. FULLY COOK GROUND BEEF
(1) 3.5 OZ. FULLY COOK PEPPERONI
(1) 5 OZ. FULLY COOKED SUMMER SAUSAGE HOT OR REGULAR
(1) 3.6 FULLY COOKED CHUNK WHITE CHICKEN
(1) 7 OZ. FULLY COOKED SHREDDED BEEF

TOAST TORTILLAS:

 LAY PAPER TOWEL INSIDE MICROWAVE WITH 1 TORTILLA ON TOP OF IT. START COOKING.

ONCE TORTILLA BEGINS TO RISE, OPEN AND PAT DOWN WITH ANOTHER PAPER TOWEL. EVERY TIME IT RAISES REPEAT.

CONTINUE THIS 2 TO 3 TIMES, THEN FLIP AND REPEAT. DO THIS UNTIL TORTILLA IS SLIGHTLY GOLDEN BROWN, FLAT, AND CRISPY. CONTINUE WITH THE REST OF THE TORTILLAS. CAREFUL DO NOT BURN.

CUT SUMMER SAUSAGE INTO SMALL CUBES. COOK FOR 1 MIN. DRAIN GREASE.

ADD GROUND BEEF, CHICKEN, AND SHREDDED BEEF IN WITH SUMMER SAUSAGE. COOK AND STIR FOR 4 MINS.

COOK PEPPERONI IN IT'S PACKAGE FOR 1 MIN.

PLACE SHARP CHEESE, AND MOZZARELLA CHEESE IN A BOWL WITH 1/4 CUP OF WATER.

COOK UNTIL CHEESE MELTS AND CREAMY, LEAVING NO CHUNKS OF CHEESE. OCCASIONALLY OPEN AND STIR TO PREVENT SPILLAGE.

LET'S BUILD OUR QUESADILLAS!

WITH 1 CREAM CHEESE, DISTRIBUTE EVENLY, USING A SPOON, ON 3 OF THE TORTILLAS.

WITH THE OTHER CREAM CHEESE, DO THE SAME ON THE OTHER 3.

REPEAT WITH PASTA SAUCE.

EVENLY DISTRIBUTE PEPPERONI ACROSS 3 TORTILLAS.

DO THE SAME WITH MEAT MIXTURE ON THE SAME 3 TORTILLAS.

REPEAT WITH MELTED CHEESE SAUCE.

WITH THE 3 REMAINING TORTILLAS, PLACE ON TOP, AND LIGHTLY PRESS DOWN.

COOK EACH QUESADILLA FOR 90 SECS.

"ENJOY YOUR MEAT LOVERS QUESADILLAS!!!"

TASTES GREAT WITH ANY KIND OF SALSA AND TORTILLA CHIPS.

SERVING SIZE:3

MEXICAN PIZZA

2 FLOUR TORTILLA SHELLS
1 RAMEN NOODLE
1 CUP OF RE-FRIED BEANS
(1) 11 OZ. CHILI W/ BEANS
1 CUP OF 'VELVEETA' SHARP CHEESE
4 OZ. MOZZARELLA CHEESE STICK
(1) 5 OZ. FULLY COOKED SUMMER SAUSAGE HOT OR REGULAR
(1) 3.5 OZ. FULLY COOKED PEPPERONI
1/2 DICED OLIVES AND JALAPENO PEPPERS MIXED
(1) 4 OZ. PASTA SAUCE

TOAST TORTILLAS:

LAY PAPER TOWEL INSIDE OF MICROWAVE AND PLACE TORTILLA ON TOP OF IT. START COOKING.
ONCE TORTILLA BEGINS TO RISE OPEN UP MICROWAVE AND PAT DOWN WITH ANOTHER PAPER TOWEL.
EVERY TIME IT RAISES REPEAT.

CONTINUE THIS 2 TO 3 TIMES, THEN FLIP AND REPEAT.
DO THIS UNTIL TORTILLA IS SLIGHTLY GOLDEN BROWN, FLAT, AND CRISPY. CAREFUL NOT TO
BURN.

CRUSH NOODLES AND PLACE IN A BOWL WITH RE-FRIED BEANS.

ADD 2 CUPS OF HOT WATER AND COOK FOR 2 MINS. THEN STIR AND LET REST.

COOK CHILI IN A SMALL BOWL FOR 2 MINS, MIX IN WITH NOODLES AND RE-FRIED BEANS.

SPREAD MIXTURE ONTO TORTILLAS EVENLY.

MELT VELVEETA CHEESE AND SPREAD EVENLY OVER MIXTURE.

DICED SUMMER SAUSAGE INTO SMALL CUBES, COOK FOR 1 MIN. DRAIN GREASE.

PLACE ON TOP OF MIXTURE AND CHEESE. PRESS DOWN LIGHTLY ON MEAT, EMERGING INTO MIXTURE.

COOK OLIVES AND JALAPENO PEPPERS FOR 30 SECS. PLACE OVER SUMMER SAUSAGE.

COOK PEPPERONI IN IT'S PACKAGE FOR 30 SECS. OPEN AND PLACE EVENLY OVER PIZZAS.

SPREAD PASTA SAUCE OVER PEPPERONI.

DICE MOZZARELLA INTO SMALL BOWL

ADD 1/4 CUP OF WATER, COOK UNTIL CHEESE HAS MELTED. OCCASIONALLY STIR AND AVOID
SPILLAGE.

ONCE CHEESE HAS MELTED AND CHEESE CHUNKS REMAIN, POUR OVER BOTH PIZZAS EVENLY.

COOK EACH PIZZA FOR 90 SECS., THEN LET REST FOR 2 MINS.

NEXT CUT PIZZA INTO 6 TO 8 SLICES.

"MMMM BOYE LETS EAT PEOPLE!!
SERVING SIZE 2

''RAJ'S FAT BOY POT PIE"

(1) 13 OZ. BOX OF 'RITZ' UNSALTED CRACKERS
(2) 11 OZ. BEEF STEW
(1) 5 OZ. FULLY COOKED SUMMER SAUSAGE HOT

DICE SUMMER SAUSAGE INTO A SMALL BOWL AND COOK FOR 1 MIN. DRAIN GREASE.

CRUSH ALL 4 ROLLS OF CRACKERS, LEAVING THEM IN THEIR PACKAGE.

TAKE 2 ROLLS AND POUR INTO A LARGE 10 LEVEL MICROWAVABLE BOWL.

TAKE 1/2 CUP OF WATER AND POUR OVER CRACKERS. MIX TOGETHER WITH HANDS INTO A BALL.
MAKE SURE EVERY CRACKER IS MIXED WELL WITH WATER. NOTE: SHOULD BE LIKE A DOUGH
TEXTURE.
IF NECESSARY, ADD A LITTLE MORE WATER.

NEXT FORM A THIN PIE CRUST INSIDE THE BOWL. CRUST SHOULD GO UP AND ALONG SIDE OF THE
BOWL.

COOK FOR 2 MINS. OR UNTIL GOLDEN BROWN. CAREFUL NOT BURN.

POUR BOTH BEEF STEWS IN A SEPARATE BOWL AND COOK FOR 2 MINS.

POUR IN OVER COOKED PIE CRUST, TOPPING WITH COOKED SUMMER SAUSAGE.

NOW REPEAT PIE CRUST DIRECTIONS BUT ONLY THIS TIME, ON A FLAT SURFACE, (PREFERABLY A
SHEET OF WAX PAPER) FLATTEN CRUST OUT IN A CIRCULAR SHAPE.

COOK FOR 90 SEC.

FLIP ONTO TOP OF POT PIE. QUICKLY, WITHOUT BREAKING IN PIECES.

WITH A FORK PINCH ALONG THE ENTIRE POT PIE LEAVING FORK MARKS. WITH A KNIFE MAKE 3
UNEVEN, SPACED OUT SLICES IN THE MIDDLE.

COOK FOR 3 MINS.

" FEEDING TIME LADIES & GENTLEMAN"

SERVING SIZE: 2 (1 FOR REALLY HUNGRY PEOPLE)

CHICKEN ALFREDO

(2) 3.6 OZ. FULLY COOKED CHUNK WHITE CHICKEN
2 'THAI PALACE' THAI RICE NOODLES
2 CREAMY CHICKEN RAMEN NOODLE SEASONING
3 TABLESPOONS OF ITALIAN SEASONING
2 TEASPOONS OF GARLIC POWDER
(2) 4 OZ. MOZZARELLA CHEESE STICKS
1/2 OF GRATED ITALIAN CHEESE
1 CUP OF MILK

ADD MOZZARELLA AND MILK TO LARGE MICROWAVABLE BOWL.

COOK ON HIGH HEAT FOR 3 MINS. OR UNTIL CHEESE IS CREAMY WITH NO CHEESE CHUNKS
REMAINING. STIR OFTEN AND AVOID SPILLAGE.

ADD GARLIC POWDER, GRATED ITALIAN CHEESE, CHICKEN, AND ITALIAN SEASONINGS.

MIX TOGETHER & COOK FOR ADDITIONAL 3 MINS.

DUST WITH ITALIAN SEASONING, AND SERVE.

"BON-APPETIT"

SERVING SIZE: 1

SMOTHERED BURRITOS

3 FLOUR TORTILLA SHELLS
1 CUP OF INSTANT WHITE RICE
1 CUP OF 'VELVEETA' CHEESE
(1) 4 OZ. MOZZARELLA CHEESE STICK
(1) 6 OZ. FULLY COOKED GROUND BEEF
(1) 5 OZ. SUMMER SAUSAGE HOT OR REGULAR
(1) 3.6 OZ. FULLY COOKED CHUNK WHITE CHICKEN
(1) 11 OZ. CHILI W/O BEANS
2 TABLESPOON OF HONEY
1/2 CUP OF DICED JALAPENO PEPPERS

ADD RICE TO A BOWL WITH 1/2 CUP OF BOILING WATER. COOK FOR 1 MIN. LET REST.

DICE SUMMER SAUSAGE INTO SMALL CUBES. COOK FOR 1MIN. DRAIN GREASE.

ADD GROUND BEEF, HONEY, DICED JALAPENO, AND CHICKEN IN WITH SAUSAGE. COOK FOR AN ADDITIONAL 3 MINS.

COOK CHILI IN A SMALL BOWL FOR 3 MINS.

ADD VELVEETA TO 1/4 CUP OF WATER AND COOK FOR 2 MINS. MELTING CHEESE AND ALLOWING IT TO BE CREAMY.

POUR VELVEETA IN WITH RICE MIXING TOGETHER.

LAY OUT THE 3 TORTILLAS AND FILL ALL 3 WITH 1/2 BOWL OF RICE AND VELVEETA.

REPEAT WITH MEAT MIXTURE.

PLACE ALL CLOSED 3 BURRITOS IN A BOWL. STACK IF NECESSARY. TOP WITH CHILI.

POUR AND SPREAD OUT REMAINING RICE OVER BURRITOS.

ADD MOZZARELLA TO A BOWL WITH1/4 CUP OF WATER AND MELT FOR 2 MINS. OR UNTIL CHEESE IS CREAMY AND NO CHEESE IS REMAINING. STIR THROUGHOUT COOKING TIME. CAREFUL NOT TO SPILL. POUR CHEESE ON TOP OF BURRITOS.

POUR MEAT MIXTURE ON TOP OF MOZZARELLA.

COOK FOR 5 MORE MINS. AND LET THEM REST FOR 5-10 MINS.

" MEAL IS COMPLETE. LET'S DIG IN!!!

SERVING SIZE: 1 (UNLESS YOU'RE FEELING GENEROUS THEN 2)

PEANUT BUTTER MEAT & RICE DISH

2 CUPS OF INSTANT WHITE RICE
1/2 CUP OF PEANUT BUTTER
1/4 CUP OF BBQ SAUCE
1 DICED DILL PICKLE
1 SUMMER SAUSAGE HOT
(1) 1/2 PK. OF 3.5 OZ. PEPPERONI
(1) 2 OZ. CRUSHED HOT & SPICY PORK RINDS

COOK RICE IN 3 CUPS OF BOILING HOT WATER. LET REST IN BOWL.

COOK SUMMER SAUSAGE, PEPPERONI, AND PICKLE IN SEPARATE BOWL FOR 3 MINS.

ADD IN BBQ SAUCE, AND PEANUT BUTTER TO MEAT MIXTURE. COOK FOR 1 MIN.

ADD IN PORK RINDS AND MIX TOGETHER.

POUR OVER RICE AND ENJOY.

"YEAHHHHH BOYEEEEE"

SERVING SIZE: 1

PIZZA POCKETS

(1) 6 PKG. OF FLOUR TORTILLA SHELL
(2) 4 OZ. PASTA SAUCE
2) TABLESPOONS OF SWEET BBQ SAUCE
(1) OZ. FULLY COOKED SHREDDED BEEF
(1) OZ. SUMMER SAUSAGE HOT
(1) 3.5 FULLY COOKED PEPPERONI
2 TABLESPOONS OF ITALIAN SEASONING
1/4 CUP OF 'VELVEETA' CHEESE
(1) 4 OZ. MOZZARELLA CHEESE STICK

DICE SUMMER SAUSAGE INTO SMALL PIECES AND ADD PEPPERONI. COOK IN LARGE MICROWAVABLE BOWL 2 MINS. DRAIN GREASE.

ADD SHREDDED BEEF, PASTA SAUCE, BBQ SAUCE, AND ITALIAN SEASONING, TO BOWL WITH SUMMER SAUSAGE. STIR AND COOK FOR 3 MINS.

COOK VELVEETA, AND MOZZARELLA IN A SEPARATE BOWL WITH 1/4 CUP OF WATER. COOK UNTIL CHEESE IS COMPLETELY MELTED, WITH NO CHEESE CHUNKS REMAINING. OCCASIONALLY STOP AND STIR. AVOID SPILLAGE.

INDIVIDUALLY HEAT EACH TORTILLA FOR 10 SECS. PLACE ON PAPER TOWELS.

ADD 3 - 4 TABLESPOONS OF PIZZA POCKET FILLING TO EACH TORTILLA.

FOLD IN 2 SIDES OF THE TORTILLA, THEN TUCK AND TIGHTLY ROLL UP PIZZA POCKET. CONTINUE WITH THE REST OF THE TORTILLAS.

ONCE FINISHED HEAT POCKETS FOR 90 SEC.

LET COOL FOR 5 MINS. AND ENJOY.

" PARTY TIME, MMMM BOYE!!!"

TASTE GREAT AS A MEAL. BUT GOES WELL WITH ANY TYPE OF CHIP.

SERVING SIZE: 3

CINNAMON FRIED RICE

(1) 7 OZ. WHITE RICE PRECOOKED OR INSTANT RICE
1 EMPTY MICROWAVE POPCORN BAG
1 'THAI PALACE' THAI RICE NOODLE
1 RAMEN NOODLE CHICKEN
(1) 5 OZ. SUMMER SAUSAGE HOT OR REGULAR
(1) 3.6 OZ. FULLY COOKED CHUNK WHITE CHICKEN
(1) 6 OZ. FILLET OF MACKEREL (IN OIL)
4 TABLE SPOONS OF SUGAR
3 TABLE SPOONS OF GROUND CINNAMON

ADD 3 CUPS OF WATER TO A LARGE MICROWAVABLE BOWL AND BOIL.

ADD THAI SEASONING, AND CHICKEN SEASONING IN WATER.

TAKE RICE AND CRUSH RAMEN AND POUR INTO POPCORN BAG.

DRAIN MACKEREL OIL INTO POPCORN BAG OVER RICE & NOODLES.

SHAKE THE BAG AND COOK ON HIGH HEAT FOR 2MINS. OCCASIONALLY OPEN MICROWAVE TO TAKE BAG
OUT & SHAKE THE RICE AROUND.

COOK ADDITIONAL 2 MINS. AFTER DOING THIS TWICE, BREAK UP THAI NOODLES & POUR IT IN
WITH RICE.

REPEAT THIS PROCESS UNTIL THE RICE & NOODLES BECOME GOLDEN BROWN. THEN POUR ENTIRE BAG
INTO THE HOT WATER. CAUTION: DON'T BURN YOURSELF. STEAM WILL BE VERY HOT.

DICE SUMMER SAUSAGE INTO SMALL PIECES.

COOK FOR 1 MIN. THEN ADD IN CHICKEN AND FISH.

SEASON MEAT WITH THAI NOODLE SEASONING. COOK FOR 5 MINS.

ADD MEAT MIXTURE, SUGAR, & CINNAMON INTO RICE AND STIR.

LET RICE REST FOR 5 MIN.

" CINNAMON RICE MY FRIEND, ENJOY!!!"

TASTE GREAT AS A MEAL, BUT GOES EVEN BETTER WITH MY FAMOUS CROQUETTES, ORANGE CHICKEN,
OR CATFISH.

SERVING SIZE: 3

ORANGE CHICKEN

(3) 3.6 OZ. FULLY COOKED CHUNK WHITE CHICKEN
3 SLEEVES OF 'RITZ' UNSALTED CRACKERS
2 CUPS OF SWEET & HOT SAUCE
1/4 CUP OF 'TANG' ORANGE DRINK MIX
HONEY
1 EMPTY MICROWAVE POPCORN BAG
UNSALTED BUTTER

PLACE CHICKEN IN A LARGE BOWL AND CRUSH 1 SLEEVE OF CRACKERS.

POUR IN OVER CHICKEN & MIX TOGETHER WITH HANDS REALLY WELL.

BEGIN TO FORM CHUNKY BITE SIZE CHICKEN NUGGETS.

CRUSH REMAINING CRACKERS AND POUR INTO A BOWL.

IN A SEPARATE BOWL POUR IN SAUCE & TANG, & MIX TOGETHER.

DRIZZLE HONEY OVER NUGGETS, COATING ALL SIDES.

ROLL EACH NUGGET IN THE CRUSHED CRACKERS.

TEAR OPEN POPCORN BAG & LAY FLAT WITH THE INSIDE OF THE BAG FACING UPWARDS. LIGHTLY
COAT THE BAG WITH BUTTER AND LAY EACH CHICKEN PIECE ON TOP.

COOK FOR 2 MINS. & FLIP OVER & COOK FOR ADDITIONAL 1 MIN. LOOK FOR LIGHT GOLDEN-BROWN
COLOR.
CAREFUL NOT TO OVER COOK, COULD HARDEN CHICKEN.

ONCE ALL CHICKEN HAS FINISHED COOKING, TOSS INTO THE SAUCE.

REMOVE & COOK FOR ANOTHER 90 SECS. ON THE SAME POPCORN BAG.

LET CHICKEN REST FOR AT LEAST 10 MINS.

" ORANGE CHICKEN IS READY FOR YOUR ENJOYMENT"

TASTE GREAT AS A MEAL, BUT GOES WELL WITH FRIED RICE, &/OR LO'MEIN

SERVING SIZE: 1

LO' MEIN

(1) 16 OZ. ANGEL HAIR PASTA
1 CUP OF MELTED BUTTER
1 TABLESPOON OF GARLIC POWDER
2 TABLESPOONS OF SUGAR
2 TABLESPOON OF SEASONING SALT

WITH A LARGE LONG MICROWAVABLE CONTAINER, FILL WITH WATER & BOIL.

WHILE BOILING, USE AN ADDITIONAL CONTAINER & PLACE PASTA IN.

COOK FOR 2 MINS. THEN OPEN MICROWAVE & WITH A LARGE SPOON OR FORK TOSS PASTA AROUND.
REPEAT.
CAREFUL NOT TO BURN. LOOK FOR PASTA TO DARKEN A LITTLE, THEN PLACE IN BOILING WATER.

COOK TIL PASTA IS TENDER, BUT NOT TOO TENDER.
NOTE: TO KNOW IF PASTA IS LO'MEIN READY, TAKE 1 NOODLE OUT OF THE WATER & TOSS IT
AGAINST THE WALL. IF IT STICKS TO THE WALL, WE'RE GOOD TO GO.

DRAIN WATER, & RINSE WITH COLD WATER THEN DRAIN AGAIN.

POUR MELTED BUTTER IN WITH THE PASTA & TOSS WITH SPOON.

COOK FOR 3 MINS., THEN STIR. REPEAT THIS 3 TIMES AND ADD IN ALL SEASONINGS.

COOK FOR 2 MORE MINS. & IT'S READY TO EAT.

ENJOY WITH ORANGE CHICKEN, SWEET & SOUR CHICKEN, FRIED RICE, OR CROQUETTES.

SERVING SIZE: 4

3 MEAT LO'MEIN W/ CHEESE & OLIVES

(1) 5 OZ. SUMMER SAUSAGE HOT OR REGULAR
(1) 3.6 OZ. FULLY COOKED CHUNK WHITE CHICKEN
(1) 6 OZ. FILLET OF MACKEREL (IN OIL)
(1) 4 OZ. MOZZARELLA CHEESE STICK
1 SERVING OF ANGEL HAIR PASTA
(1) 2.3 OZ. PKG. OF OLIVES
1 TEASPOON OF GARLIC POWDER
1 TEASPOON OF MRS. DASH SEASONING

BOIL LARGE BOWL OF WATER & ADD PASTA.

COOK FOR 3 MINS. THEN DRAIN WATER.

RINSE WITH COLD WATER & DRAIN AGAIN.

FOLLOW UP WITH DRAINING MACKEREL OIL OVER PASTA.

STIR & FRY NOODLES FOR 3 MINS.

DICE SUMMER SAUSAGE & COOK FOR 1 MIN. DRAIN GREASE.

LAY SAUSAGE STRAIGHT DOWN THE MIDDLE OF THE BOWL ON TOP OF THE NOODLES.

COOK CHICKEN FOR 2 MINS. THEN LAY ON THE RIGHT SIDE OF BOWL NEXT TO THE SAUSAGE.

COOK MACKEREL FOR 3 MINS. CAREFUL FISH WILL POP WHEN HOT. WHEN FINISHED LAY ON THE LEFT SIDE OF SAUSAGE.

COOK MOZZARELLA, & DICED OLIVES IN A BOWL WITH 1/4 CUP OF WATER UNTIL CHEESE IS MELTED, LEAVING NO CHUNKS OF CHEESE.

ADD GARLIC AND MRS. DASH IN WITH CHEESE.

POUR EVENLY OVER ALL MEAT. COOK DISH FOR 3 MORE MINS. AND ENJOY.

"DINNER IS SERVED!!!"

SERVING SIZE: 1

FISH BURRITOS

(2) 6 OZ. FILLET OF MACKEREL (IN OIL)
1/4 CUP OF SPANISH RICE PRE-COOKED
3 FLOUR TORTILLA SHELL
1/4 OF DICED JALAPENO PEPPERS
(1) 4 OZ. MOZZARELLA CHEESE
1 TABLESPOON IN SEASONING SALT

DRAIN FISH OIL FROM MACKEREL.

COOK MACKEREL AND JALAPENO FOR 3 MINS. BE SURE TO COVER WITH LID. FISH WILL POP WHEN HOT.

ADD 1 CUP OF HOT WATER TO RICE & COOKED FOR 3 MINS. THEN ADD IN FISH & STIR.

MELT MOZZARELLA WITH 1/4 CUP OF WATER UNTIL CHEESE IS CREAMY LEAVING NO CHUNKS OF CHEESE.

POUR CHEESE IN WITH RICE & FISH. STIR TOGETHER & COOK FOR 4 MINS.

HEAT TORTILLA SHELLS INDIVIDUALLY FOR 10 SECS. A PIECE.

NEXT ADD FILLING TO EACH SHELL, DISTRIBUTING EVENLY.

FOLD IN A BURRITO STYLE, THEN TOAST EACH ONE IN A TOASTER.

"YUM, YUM, GET CHA SOME!!!

SERVING SIZE: 1

3 CHEESE MAC & CHEESE

(1) 16 OZ. BAG OF ELBOW NOODLES
1 PKG. OF CREAMY CHICKEN RAMEN NOODLE SEASONING
(2) 4 OZ. MOZZARELLA CHEESE STICK
1/2 CUP OF 'VELVEETA' CHEESE
(2) 2 OZ. PKG. OF CREAM CHEESE
1/2 CUP OF MILK
1 TABLESPOON OF SUGAR

BOIL LARGE BOWL OF WATER. THEN ADD IN NOODLES.

COOK UNTIL NOODLES BECOME TENDER, THEN DRAIN WATER & RINSE WITH COLD WATER.

ADD ALL CHEESES IN A LARGE MICROWAVABLE BOWL WITH MILK, SUGAR, & CHICKEN SEASONING.

MELT UNTIL CHEESE IS CREAMY & HAVING NO CHEESE CHUNKS REMAINING.

ADD CHEESE TO NOODLES & STIR IN.

COOK MAC & CHEESE FOR 10 MINS.

"LET'S EAT."

SERVING SIZE: 5

CHEESEBURGER EGG ROLLS

(1) 6 OZ. FULLY COOKED GROUND BEEF
1/4 CUP OF DICED DILL PICKLE
1 TEASPOON OF 'LAWRY'S' SEASONING SALT
(1) 6 PKG. OF FLOUR TORTILLA SHELLS
(1) 4 OZ. MOZZARELLA CHEESE STICK
1/2 CUP OF 'VELVEETA' CHEESE
1/2 CUP OF FRIED ONIONS OR MINCED ONIONS
2 TABLESPOONS OF BLACK PEPPER
2 TABLESPOONS OF UNSALTED BUTTER

EMPTY GROUND BEEF IN A LARGE MICROWAVABLE BOWL & COOK FOR 4 MINS. DRAIN GREASE.

STIR IN ALL SEASONINGS.

IN A SEPARATE BOWL, FRY ONIONS WITH BUTTER FOR 2 MINS. WHEN DONE TOSS IN WITH GROUND BEEF.

MELT BOTH CHEESES TOGETHER IN A BOWL WITH 1/4 CUP OF WATER.

MELT UNTIL CHEESE IS CREAMY WITH CHUNKS REMAINING.

POUR CHEESE & DICED PICKLE IN WITH GROUND BEEF.

STIR & COOK FOR 3 MINS.

USE A MICROWAVABLE BOWL LID TO HEAT TORTILLAS.

TAKE ONE TORTILLA & WET YOUR HAND, THEN GENTLY RUB WATER ONTO BOTH SIDES OF THE TORTILLA.

HEAT FOR 10 SECS. ON ONE SIDE, THEN FLIP OVER & REPEAT FOR 5 MORE SECS.

FILL THE MIDDLE OF TORTILLA WITH 3 TABLESPOONS OF GROUND BEEF FILLING.

FOLD IN TWO SIDES OF THE TORTILLA, TUCK & ROLL IN OTHER SIDE TIGHTLY AS IF ROLLING UP A BURRITO.

RIGHT BEFORE COMPLETELY CLOSING THE EGG ROLL, WET FINGER TIPS, & LIGHTLY WET THE EDGE. SEALING UP THE ROLL.

REPEAT WITH ALL 6 TORTILLAS.

HEAT ALL EGG ROLLS FOR 30 SECS. EACH.

Lettuce, and tomato goes very well with this also!

"TIME TO GET DOWN WIT THE GET DOWN!!!"

DIPPING SAUCE SUGGESTIONS: KETCHUP & MUSTARD MIX, MAYO, &/OR BBQ SAUCE.
GOES GREAT WITH FRIES, OR CHIPS.

SERVING SIZE: 2

MASHED POTATOES MADE W/ SOUR CREAM & ONION POTATO CHIPS

(3) 6 OZ. BAGS OF SOUR CREAM & ONION POTATO CHIPS.
2 CUPS OF MILK
1/4 CUP OF UNSALTED BUTTER

SMASH CHIPS WHILE STILL IN THEIR BAG.

POUR ALL THE CRUSHED CHIPS INTO 1 BAG.

HEAT MILK WITH BUTTER FOR 2 MINS. THEN POUR INTO BAG WITH CHIPS.

MIX TOGETHER WELL BY SQUEEZING THE OUTSIDE OF THE BAG. ADD MORE MILK IF REQUIRED.

POUR THE POTATOES IN A LARGE BOWL & COOK FOR 3-5 MINS. STIR THROUGHOUT COOKING TIME.

COOK UNTIL POTATOES ARE NICE & FLUFFY.

ADD DESIRED AMOUNT OF BUTTER WHEN COMPLETED.

ENJOY.

SERVING SIZE: 3-5

BIG RAJ'S HOMEMADE CHILI

(1) 11 OZ. HOT CHILI
(1) 11 OZ. REGULAR CHILI
(1) 10 OZ. BLACK BEANS
(1) 6 OZ. FULLY COOKED GROUND BEEF
(1) 7 OZ. FULLY COOKED SHREDDED BEEF
1 RAMEN CHILI SEASONING
1 TEASPOON OF GARLIC POWDER
3 TABLESPOONS OF HONEY
1 RED CASERA SALSA
1 CUP OF SHREDDED MOZZARELLA CHEESE
1/2 CUP OF 'VELVEETA' CHEESE

EMPTY BOTH PKGS. OF CHILI IN A LARGE MICROWAVE BOWL.

RINSE BLACKS BEANS IN A STRAINER, THEN PUT IN CHILI.

COOK FOR 3 MINS.

PLACE ALL MEATS IN A BOWL & COOK FOR 3 MINS.

POUR MEAT IN WITH CHILI, ALONG WITH HONEY, SEASONING, & VELVEETA CHEESE. COOK FOR 5 MINS.

STIR IN RED CASERA SALSA & COOK FOR ANOTHER 3 MINS.

TOP CHILI WITH SHREDDED MOZZARELLA.

ENJOY.

TASTE GREAT WITH SOUR CREAM AND 'RITZ' CRACKERS.

CHILI CHEESE SLIDERS

6 PKG. OF FLOUR TORTILLA SHELLS
(2) 5 OZ. SUMMER SAUSAGE HOT OR REGULAR
(1)11 OZ. REGULAR CHILI
1 CUP OF 'VELVEETA' CHEESE
2 TABLESPOONS OF HONEY

DICE SUMMER SAUSAGE INTO SMALL PIECES. COOK FOR 2 MINS. & DRAIN GREASE.

POUR CHILI, HONEY, & CHEESE IN WITH SAUSAGE & COOK FOR 4 MORE MINS.

HEAT TORTILLAS FOR 15 SECS.

FILL EACH TORTILLA WITH 1/2 OF CUP OF MIXTURE THEN WRAP & ROLL INTO A BURRITO.

TASTE GREAT AS A MEAL, EVEN BETTER WITH CHIPS.

SERVING SIZE: 2

FRIED RICE

(1) 5 OZ. SUMMER SAUSAGE HOT OR REGULAR
(1) 3.6 OZ. OF CHUNK WHITE CHICKEN
(1) 3.7 OZ. 'THAI PALACE' THAI RICE NOODLE
(1) 6 OZ. FILLET OF MACKEREL (IN OIL)
1 RAMEN NOODLE
1 CUP OF INSTANT WHITE RICE
1 USED POPCORN BAG

BOIL A LARGE BOWL OF 4 TO 5 CUPS OF WATER & ADD IN THAI NOODLE SEASONING.

PLACE RICE & CRUSHED UP RAMEN IN THE POPCORN BAG.

DICE SUMMER SAUSAGE IN SMALL PIECES & COOK FOR 2 MINS. DRAIN GREASE.

DRAIN MACKEREL OIL OVER RICE & NOODLES THEN SHAKE THE BAG UP & COOK FOR 2 MINS. THEN SHAKE THE BAG UP AGAIN, & COOK FOR ANOTHER 2 MINS.

CRUSH THAI NOODLES & PUT IT IN THE BAG WITH RICE. COOK UNTIL EVERYTHING IS GOLDEN BROWN. CAREFUL NOT TO BURN.

ONCE DONE COOKING POUR INTO BOWL OF HOT SEASONED WATER. CAREFUL STREAM WILL BE EXTREMELY HOT.

STIR & COOK FOR 3 MINS.

ADD CHICKEN AND MACKEREL IN WITH SUMMER SAUSAGE, COOK FOR 3 MINS.

LAST POUR MEAT IN WITH RICE & NOODLES. LET IT REST FOR 10 MINS.

"STIR & ENJOY FOLKS!!!"

*SUGGESTED SAUCES: SOY OR SWEET & HOT

SERVING SIZE: 3

GARLIC TOAST

4 SLICES OF BREAD
BUTTER
GARLIC POWDER
1 USED POPCORN BAG

BUTTER BOTH SIDES OF THE BREAD.

CUT OPEN THE POPCORN BAG & LAY FLAT WITH THE INSIDE OF THE BAG FACING IN A UPWARD
POSITION.

LAY BREAD DOWN ON TOP OF THE BAG & THEN LIGHTLY DUST THE BREAD WITH GARLIC POWDER.

COOK UNTIL BREAD IS TOASTED.

TASTE GREAT WITH SPAGHETTI OR LASAGNA.

SERVING SIZE: 2

TUNA MELT

(2) 4 OZ. PKG. OF TUNA
2 TABLESPOONS OF DICED DILL PICKLE
1 TEASPOON OF SUGAR
3 TABLESPOONS OF MAYO
2 TEASPOONS OF MUSTARD
2 PLAIN BAGELS
4 SLICES OF CHEESE
1 USED POPCORN BAG
BUTTER

MIX TUNA, MUSTARD, MAYO, PICKLE, & SUGAR INTO A BOWL.

TEAR OPEN POPCORN BAG WITH THE INSIDE OF THE BAG FACING IN AN UPWARD POSITION.

BUTTER EACH BAGEL ON BOTH SIDES LIGHTLY & COOK ON BOTH SIDES UNTIL GOLDEN BROWN.

PLACE ONE SLICE OF CHEESE ON EACH BAGEL.

ASSEMBLE SANDWICHES.

COOK SANDWICHES IN THE MICROWAVE FOR 90 SECS. EACH.

SLICE SANDWICHES IN HALF & ENJOY.

TASTE GREAT WITH CHIPS.

SERVING SIZE: 2

BREAD STICKS OR GARLIC KNOTS

3 PLAIN BAGELS
GARLIC
1/2 SLEEVE OF SALTINE CRACKERS
BUTTER
ITALIAN SEASONING

BREAK UP BAGELS & CRACKERS IN A LARGE BOWL.

ADD 1 CUP OF WARM WATER & MIX WITH HANDS.

ADD MORE WATER IF NEEDED. WE WANT IT TO HAVE A DOUG- LIKE TEXTURE.

BEGIN TO FORM BREAD STICKS OR KNOTS.

COOK FOR 2 MINS IN THE MICROWAVE. LONGER
IF DOUGH FEELS DAMP.

SPREAD BUTTER ON TOP OF BREAD STICKS OR KNOTS, & DUST WITH ITALIAN & GARLIC
SEASONINGS.

COOK FOR 1 MORE MIN.

"MMMmmm BOY, LET'S EAT!!!"

TASTES GREAT WITH SPAGHETTI OR LASAGNA.

CHILI CHEESE HOT FRIES

(1) 8 OZ. BAG OF FLAMIN HOT CHEETOS
(1) 11 OZ. PKG. OF CHILI
1 CUP OF 'VELVEETA' CHEESE

POUR BAG OF CHEETOS INTO A LARGE BOWL.

HEAT CHILI & MIX IN WITH CHEETOS.

HEAT CHEESE & POUR OVER CHILI & CHEETOS.

ALLOW TO SIT AWHILE TO SOFTEN FRIES.

"THEN HEAT & EAT!!!"

SERVING SIZE: 2

CALZONE

10 PLAIN BAGELS
(2) 6 OZ. FULLY COOKED GROUND BEEF
(1) 5 OZ. SUMMER SAUSAGE HOT OR REGULAR
(1) 3.5 OZ. PEPPERONI
(2) 4 OZ. PASTA SAUCES
(2) TABLESPOONS OF ITALIAN SEASONING
1 CUP OF 'VELVEETA' CHEESE
(1) 4 OZ. MOZZARELLA CHEESE STICK
UNSALTED BUTTER

BREAK UP ALL BAGELS & PLACE THEM IN A LARGE BOWL.

POUR 2 CUPS OF WARM WATER OVER BAGELS.

ADD MORE WATER AS YOU GO IF NEEDED.

MIX TOGETHER WITH HANDS FORMING A DOUGH. AGAIN USE MORE WATER IF NEEDED.

FLATTEN DOUGH OUT THINLY ONTO WAX PAPER IN A CIRCULAR SHAPE.

COOK FOR 3 MINS ON HIGH HEAT. SHOULD BE NICE & DRY WHEN DONE COOKING. IF NOT, COOK FOR ANOTHER MINUTE OR SO.

SPREAD PASTA SAUCE ON EVENLY.

MELT VELVEETA CHEESE & SPREAD EVENLY OVER PASTA SAUCE.

DICE SUMMER SAUSAGE & COOK FOR 2 MINS. DRAIN GREASE.

ADD IN GROUND BEEF & COOK FOR 3 MORE MINS.

COOK PEPPERONI IN IT'S PKG. FOR 1 MIN. & LAY IT OUT ON ONE SIDE OF THE CALZONE DOUGH.

POUR GROUND BEEF & SUMMER SAUSAGE OVER PEPPERONI.

SLICE UP MOZZARELLA, PLACE IN A BOWL, ADDING 1/4 CUP OF WATER.

COOK UNTIL CREAMY, LEAVING NO CHUNKS OF CHEESE. OPEN MICROWAVE & STIR CONSTANTLY, TO AVOID SPILLAGE.

POUR CHEESE OVER THE WHOLE CALZONE. THEN FOLD OVER THE DOUGH THAT DOESN'T HAVE MEAT ON TOP, SEALING THE CALZONE.

USING A KNIFE, LEAVE INDENTS ALONG THE EDGE OF THE CALZONE.

SPREAD BUTTER THINLY ON TOP & LIGHTLY DUST ITALIAN SEASONING OVER THE BUTTER.

COOK CALZONE FOR 3 MINS. & LET IT REST FOR 10 MINS.

CUT SLICES TO YOUR LIKING.

" PERFECT FOR SUNDAY FOOTBALL!!!"

SERVING SIZE: 4

BIG RAJ'S RICE DISH W/ MMM BOYE SAUCE

2 CUPS OF INSTANT WHITE RICE
(1) 5 OZ. SUMMER SAUSAGE HOT OR REGULAR
(1) 3.5 OZ. PEPPERONI
(1) 6 OZ. FILLET OF MACKEREL (IN OIL)
(1) CALIFORNIA VEGETABLE CUP SOUP
1/4 CUP OF SOY SAUCE
1 RAMEN NOODLE W/O SEASONING
1/4 CUP BBQ SAUCE
1/2 CUP OF PEANUT BUTTER
DASH OF PEPPER, SALT, GARLIC POWDER, & HOT SAUCE
2 TABLESPOONS OF FRENCH DRESSING
1/4 OF CRUSHED PEANUTS
1 USED MICROWAVE POPCORN BAG

BOIL A LARGE BOWL OF WATER.

EMPTY RICE & NOODLES (CRUSH UP NOODLES) INTO POPCORN BAG, & DRAIN MACKEREL OIL ONTO IT.

SHAKE THE BAG UP & COOK UNTIL GOLDEN BROWN. NOTE: SHAKE UP BAG THROUGHOUT COOKING TIME & CAREFUL NOT TO BURN.

POUR RICE & NOODLES INTO THE HOT WATER. CAREFUL STREAM WILL BE HOT.

CUT SUMMER SAUSAGE INTO LARGE CHUNKS. COOK FOR 2 MINS. DRAIN GREASE.

ADD PEPPERONI, MACKEREL, PEANUT BUTTER, ALL SEASONINGS, BBQ SAUCE, HOT SAUCE, & FRENCH DRESSING.

COOK FOR 5 MINS. AND STIR IN BETWEEN COOKING TIME.

ADD HOT WATER IN CUP SOUP.

COOK UNTIL NOODLES SOFTEN, DRAIN WATER, THEN ADD TO FRIED RICE & RAMEN NOODLE.

MIX TOGETHER ADDING SOY SAUCE. COOK FOR 3 MINS.

ADD PEANUTS IN WITH MEAT & SAUCE MIXTURE.

POUR OVER RICE & NOODLES. COOK FOR 3 MINS.

"ENJOY PEOPLE!!!"

SERVING SIZE: 2

CHICKEN PARMESAN

(3) 3.6 OZ. OF FULLY COOKED CHUNK WHITE CHICKEN
2 SLEEVES OF 'RITZ' UNSALTED CRACKERS
1 SERVING OF ANGEL HAIR PASTA
(2) 4 OZ. PASTA SAUCES
(1) 4 OZ. MOZZARELLA CHEESE STICKS
1 TABLESPOON OF ITALIAN SEASONING
1 TABLESPOON OF GARLIC POWDER
HONEY
UNSALTED BUTTER
1 USED POPCORN BAG

BOIL A BOWL OF HOT WATER & COOK PASTA. FOLLOW COOKING DIRECTIONS.

PLACE CHICKEN IN A BOWL AND MIX IN 1/2 SLEEVE OF CRUSHED UP CRACKERS.

MIX TOGETHER WITH HANDS, THEN FORM PATTIES.

CRUSH THE OTHER SLEEVE & PLACE IN A BOWL WITH THE OTHER HALF.

NEXT DRIZZLE HONEY ONTO CHICKEN, FULLY COATING BOTH SIDES.

COAT WITH CRUSHED CRACKERS.

OPEN POPCORN BAG & LAY FLAT WITH THE INSIDE OF THE BAG FACING IN AN UPWARD POSITION.

LIGHTLY SPREAD BUTTER ONTO THE INSIDE OF THE BAG, THEN PLACE CHICKEN DOWN.

COOK FOR 3 MINS. THEN FLIP OVER & COOK FOR AN ADDITIONAL 2 MINS. OR UNTIL GOLDEN BROWN.

PLACE CHICKEN PATTIES ON TOP OF PASTA.

HEAT PASTA SAUCE & POUR OVER CHICKEN & PASTA.

MELT MOZZARELLA, GARLIC POWDER, & ITALIAN SEASONING IN A BOWL WITH 1/4 CUP OF WATER. MAKE SURE THAT NO CHEESE CHUNKS IS LEFT IN WITH MELTED CHEESE.

POUR OVER PASTA SAUCE.

HEAT FOR 2 MORE MINS. & SERVE WITH GARLIC BREAD.

"TIME TO EAT MY FRIEND!!!"

SERVING SIZE: 2

CHICKEN FRIED STEAK

(3) 3.6 OZ. FULLY COOKED CHUNK WHITE CHICKEN
 SLEEVES OF 'RITZ' UNSALTED CRACKERS
BUTTER
HONEY
2 TABLESPOONS OF BLACK PEPPER
1 TABLESPOON OF LAWRY'S SEASONING SALT
1 USED POPCORN BAG

MIX TOGETHER WITH HANDS CHICKEN & 1/2 A SLEEVE OF CRUSHED CRACKERS.
THEN FORM CHICKEN PATTIES.

NEXT CRUSH THE REMAINING CRACKERS INTO A BOWL & ADD IN SEASONING SALT.

COAT PATTIES WITH HONEY & BREAD THEM IN CRUSHED UP CRACKERS.

RIP OPEN THE POPCORN BAG & LAY FLAT WITH THE INSIDE OF BAG FACING IN A UPWARD
POSITION.

SPREAD BUTTER ONTO BAG.

FRY CHICKEN FOR 3 MINS. THEN FLIP & COOK FOR ANOTHER 2 MINS. OR UNTIL CHICKEN IS
GOLDEN BROWN.

DUST WITH BLACK PEPPER.

ENJOY.

*TASTE GREAT WITH MY MASHED POTATOES & GRAVY.

SERVING SIZE: 2

DEEP DISH BOWL PIZZA

3 FLOUR TORTILLA SHELLS
(2) 4 OZ. MOZZARELLA CHEESE STICKS
(1) 2.3 OZ. PKG. OF OLIVES
(1) 5 OZ SUMMER SAUSAGE HOT OR REGULAR
(1) 3.5 OZ PEPPERONI
(1) 4 OZ. PKG. OF PASTA SAUCE

CUT THIN SLICES OF MOZZARELLA CHEESE & PLACE IN A BOWL.

DICE SUMMER SAUSAGE INTO SMALL PIECES. COOK FOR 2 MINS. DRAIN GREASE.

COOK PEPPERONI IN IT'S PKG. FOR 1 MIN.

USING A LARGE TORTILLA SIZE BOWL, PLACE 1 TORTILLA IN IT.

SPREAD 1/3 OF THE PKG. OF PASTA SAUCE ON THE TORTILLA.

SPREAD SOME OF THE MOZZARELLA ON TOP.

LAY OUT 1/3 OF PEPPERONI, OLIVES, & SUMMER SAUSAGE.

FOLLOW UP WITH ANOTHER TORTILLA.

REPEAT TWICE: PASTA SAUCE, MOZZARELLA, PEPPERONI, OLIVES, SUMMER SAUSAGE, & A TORTILLA.

ONCE THE PIZZA IS BUILT, COOK FOR 6 MINS. HIGH HEAT.

LET THE PIZZA REST FOR 10 MINS. AT LEAST.

SLICE INTO 4 PIECES & SERVE.

ENJOY!!!

SERVING SIZE: 1

"JUICY LUCY" FISH SANDWICH

(1) 6 OZ. FILLET OF MACKEREL (IN OIL)
1/2 SLEEVE OF CRUSHED 'RITZ' UNSALTED CRACKERS
1 HEAPING SPOON OF DICED JALAPENO PEPPERS
A DASH OF SEASONING SALT & BLACK PEPPER
2 TABLESPOONS OF UNSALTED BUTTER
1/3 BLOCK OF 4 OZ. MOZZARELLA CHEESE STICK
1 PLAIN BAGEL
1 TABLESPOON OF HOT SAUCE

MIX MACKEREL, JALAPENO PEPPERS, & CRUSHED CRACKERS IN A BOWL USING YOUR HANDS.

ADD SALT & PEPPER.

FORM 2 PATTIES, THINLY SLICE CHEESE & PLACE IN THE MIDDLE OF THE PATTIE.

PLACE THE SECOND PATTIE ON TOP & MASH TOGETHER.

SPREAD BUTTER ON BOTH SIDES.

COOK FOR 2 MIMS. THEN FLIP OVER & COOK FOR ANOTHER 2 MINS. OR UNTIL THE PATTIE BECOMES GOLDEN BROWN.

POUR HOT SAUCE ON TOP & COOK FOR ANOTHER 1 MIN.

HEAT BAGEL FOR 10 SECS. & BUILD SANDWICH.

DESERTS

CUPCAKES WITH STRAWBERRY CREAM CHEESE FROSTING

(2) 16 OZ BAGS OF VANILLA WAFERS

(1) 20 OZ. COKE SODA

(2) 6 OZ. BAGS OF FRENCH VANILLA COFFEE CREAMER

2 SINGLE 'CRUSH' STRAWBERRY KOOL-AID PKGS.

(5) 2 OZ. CREAM CHEESE PKG.

BUTTER

CRUSH COOKIES UP & PLACE IN A LARGE MIXING BOWL.

POUR SODA OVER COOKIES & MIX TOGETHER WELL FORMING A CAKE BATTER.

PUT CREAM CHEESE IN A BOWL & MIX IN THE KOOL-AID SINGLES & COFFEE CREAMER.

IF YOU HAVE A MICROWAVABLE CUPCAKE BAKING PAN GREAT, USE IT.

IF NOT, A 22 OZ. PLASTIC COFFEE CUP WILL WORK FINE.

GREASE THE PAN OR CUP WITH BUTTER. THEN POUR 1 CUP OF BATTER IN & COOK FOR 2-3 MINS.

ONCE THE CUPCAKES LOOKS LIKE THEY'RE DONE, STICK A BUTTER KNIFE IN THE MIDDLE OF IT. IF THE KNIFE COMES OUT CLEAN, THEN IT'S DONE. IF NOT COOK FOR ANOTHER MINUTE OR SO.

LET THE CUPCAKES COOL DOWN THEN POP THEM OUT OF THE PAN OR CUP & APPLY DESIRED AMOUNT OF FROSTING.

"ANYONE HAVE A SWEET TOOTH?"

SERVING SIZE: 1 CUPCAKE PER PERSON

RAJ'S 5 STAR HOMEMADE APPLE PIE

(1) 16 OZ. BAG OF VANILLA WAFERS

1 TABLESPOON OF SUGAR

2 CUPS OF BUTTER

15 APPLES

1/2 CUP OF CINNAMON

(1) 3 OZ. BAG OF CARAMELS

1/4 CUP OF CRUSHED PECANS

1 CUP OF SYRUP

COMPLETELY PEEL ALL THE APPLES, REMOVE THE CORE, & SLICE IN THIN PIECES. RINSE WITH COLD WATER, THEN DRAIN.

MIX CINNAMON & SYRUP IN WITH APPLES. COOK FOR 15 MINS. OR UNTIL APPLES ARE SLIGHTLY SOFTENED.

NEXT CRUSH COOKIES IN IT'S PKG. THEN PLACE 1/3 OF THE COOKIES IN A 10 LEVEL BOWL & THE REST IN A SEPARATE 10 LEVEL BOWL.

POUR SUGAR EVENLY IN BOTH BOWLS WITH COOKIES.

IN THE BOWL WITH THE MOST COOKIES, PUT 1 CUP & 1/3 OF BUTTER IN & MIX.

PUT THE REST OF THE BUTTER IN WITH THE LEAST AMOUNT OF COOKIES.

COOK BOWL WITH THE MOST COOKIES FOR 2-3 MINS, THEN WITH A SPOON BEGIN TO FORM A PIE CRUST.

CONTINUE THE COOKING PROCESS UNTIL THERE'S A GOLDEN BROWN COLOR TO THE CRUST. NOTE: YOU WILL HAVE TO STOP THE COOKING PROCESS & FORM CRUST OCCASIONALLY. CAREFUL NOT TO BURN.

WITH THE OTHER BOWL DO THE SAME ONLY KEEP THE CRUST FLAT IN THE BOWL.

POUR APPLES IN WITH THE CRUST THAT HAS THE MOST COOKIES.

FLIP THE CRUST WITH THE LEAST AMOUNT OF COOKIES OVER ON TOP OF THE PIE. TAP THE BOTTOM OF THE BOWL TO GET ALL THE CRUST OUT. CRUST WILL BE BROKEN UP. THAT'S OK! JUST SPREAD IT OUT OVER THE APPLES EVENLY.

PLACE CARAMEL IN A BOWL WITH 2 TABLESPOONS OF BUTTER & MELT IN THE MICROWAVE. CAREFUL, STIR OFF & ON TO AVOID SPILLAGE & PROPERLY MELT CARAMEL. PLACE CRUSHED PECANS IN WITH CARAMEL & POUR OVER PIE.

"ENJOY!!!"

SERVING SIZE: 8

PEANUT BUTTER COOKIES

(1) 16 OZ. BAG OF VANILLA COOKIES

1 CUP OF MELTED PEANUT BUTTER

1/4 - CUP OF COLD BUTTER

2 TABLESPOONS OF SUGAR

1/2 - CUP OF MELTED CARAMEL

CRUSH COOKIES IN IT'S PKG. TO A FINE POWDER & POUR INTO A LARGE BOWL.

MIX IN PEANUT BUTTER, SUGAR, COLD BUTTER, & CARAMEL WITH HANDS REALLY WELL.

LAY OUT A SHEET OF WAX PAPER THAT WILL FIT NICELY IN YOUR MICROWAVE. MAY HAVE TO USE 2 TO 3 PIECES OF PAPER.

BEGIN TO FORM YOUR COOKIES.

ONCE THEY ARE MADE, USING A WET FORK, GENTLY PRESS THE FORK DOWN ONTO EACH COOKIE. THIS WILL LEAVE FORK MARKS ACROSS THE COOKIE. PRESS DOWN IN ONE DIRECTION, THEN AGAIN ACROSS THE THOSE MARKS.

COOK FOR 2 1/2 MINS. & LET COOL FOR 15 MINS.

" TASTES GREAT WITH A BIG GLASS OF MILK!!!"

SERVING SIZE: 6-8

PEANUT BRITTLE

(1) 3 OZ. BAG OF VANILLA CARAMELS

(1) 2.5 OZ. OF HONEY ROASTED PEANUTS

1 HEAPING TABLESPOON OF BUTTER

1 USED PLASTIC CHIP BAG (LARGE)

COLD & WET TOWELS

CUT OPEN CHIP BAG & LAY FLAT WITH THE INSIDE FACING IN AN UPWARD POSITION. CLEAN BAG OF ANY LEFTOVER CHIPS.

LAY COLD TOWEL UNDER BAG.

PLACE CARAMEL IN A SMALL CEREAL BOWL WITH BUTTER.

COOK & STIR OFTEN UNTIL MELTED. BE CAREFUL OF SPILLAGE.

ONCE MELTED ADD PEANUTS.

COOK UNTIL CARAMEL BECOMES SLIGHTLY DARKER THAN ORIGINAL COLOR.

POUR ONTO ONE HALF OF THE CHIP BAG. FOLD OVER OTHER HALF ON TOP OF CARAMEL.

PLACE ANOTHER COLD TOWEL ON TOP OF BAG & LIGHTLY PAT DOWN WITH BOTH HANDS UNTIL IT HARDENS.

LET COOL FOR TEN MINUTES, THEN BREAK INTO PIECES & ENJOY.

SERVING SIZE: 2

BIG RAJ'S CAKE PIE

(1) 14 OZ. DUPLEX SANDWICH COOKIES

(2) 3 OZ. CARAMELS

(1) 2.5 OZ. HONEY ROASTED PEANUTS (CRUSHED)

2 TABLESPOONS OF BUTTER

USING A 10 LEVEL MICROWAVABLE BOWL, SEPARATE ENOUGH COOKIES TO LAY FLAT IN THE BOTTOM OF THE BOWL. SET ASIDE THE OTHER HALF.

WITH THE REMAINING WHOLE COOKIES BREAK INTO SMALL CHUNKS & ADD CRUSHED PEANUTS.

MELT BOTH BAGS OF CARAMEL WITH BUTTER. CAREFUL NOT TO SPILL.

POUR HALF OF THE MELTED CARAMEL IN WITH CRUSHED COOKIES & PEANUTS. MIX WELL & POUR OVER COOKIES IN THE BOWL. LAY EVENLY COVERING EACH COOKIE.

TOP OFF WITH THE HALF THAT WAS SAT ASIDE.

POUR REMAINING CARAMEL OVER ENTIRE PIE.

LET SIT FOR AT LEAST AN HOUR.

"CUT IN 8 SLICES & DIVE IN HEAD-FIRST!!!"

SERVING SIZE: 4

BUTTER FINGER & PEANUT CARAMEL POPCORN BALLS

(2) BAGS OF MICROWAVE POPCORN

2 BUTTER FINGER CANDY BARS

(4) 3 OZ. BAGS OF CARAMELS

(1) 2.5 OZ. OF HONEY ROASTED PEANUTS

6 TABLESPOONS OF BUTTER

POP POPCORN & POUR INTO A LARGE MIXING BOWL

CRUSH UP CANDY BARS & PEANUTS. ADD IN WITH POPCORN.

MELT CARAMELS WITH BUTTER & POUR WITH POPCORN. MIX IN WITH BOTH HANDS.

FORM MIXTURE INTO POPCORN BALLS & LET SIT FOR 10 MINS.

"WHAT TIME IS IT??? SNACK THIRTY!!!"

SERVING SIZE: 6

PEANUT BUTTER CHOCOLATE RED VELVET CAKE

(2) 16 OZ. BAGS OF VANILLA WAFERS

(2) 9 OZ. BAGS OF HOT COCOA

(1) 20 OZ. SODA COKE

2 'CRUSH' STRAWBERRY SINGLE PKGS.

1 CUP OF PEANUT BUTTER (MELTED)

2 HERSHEY CANDY BARS

2 CUPS OF CRUSHED PEANUTS

CRUSH COOKIES IN ITS PKG.

POUR 1 BAG IN A 10 LEVEL MICROWAVABLE BOWL. THEN THE OTHER BAG IN ANOTHER 10 LEVEL BOWL.

POUR SODA IN BOTH BOWLS EQUALLY. ADD SINGLE PKGS IN EACH BOWL & STIR INTO CAKE BATTER.

POUR HOT COCOA MIX & MELTED PEANUT BUTTER IN A LARGE BOWL. MIX TOGETHER INTO A FROSTING. IF IT'S TO THICK ADD A LITTLE WATER TO THIN OUT.

COOK EACH CAKE UNTIL IT RISES. USE BUTTER KNIFE BY STICKING IT IN THE MIDDLE OF CAKE. IF IT COMES OUT CLEAN, IT'S DONE.

LET CAKES REST FOR 15 MIN. THEN DUMP ONTO A FLAT SURFACE BY FLIPPING IT OVER REALLY FAST & TAPPING THE BOTTOM OF THE BOWL. THEN SPREAD FROSTING OVER THE TOP.

NEXT DO THE SAME WITH THE SECOND CAKE. FLIP IT OVER ON TOP OF THE FIRST CAKE. SPREAD FROSTING OVER THE ENTIRE CAKE.

LAST APPLY PEANUTS & CRUSHED HERSHEY BAR IN WHICH EVER WAY YOU DESIRE.

" GREAT FOR BIRTHDAYS &/OR OTHER SPECIAL OCCASIONS!!!"

SERVING SIZE: 10

BANANA PUDDING

3 BANANAS

(1) 16 OZ. BAG OF VANILLA WAFERS

2 SINGLE PKGS. OF REGULAR INSTANT OATMEAL

3 SINGLE PKGS. OF 'BANANAS & CREAM INSTANT OATMEAL'

1/4 CUP OF SUGAR

1/2 CUP OF BUTTER

EMPTY OUT ALL OATMEAL PKGS. INTO A BOWL & FOLLOW COOKING DIRECTIONS FOR WATER AMOUNT.

ADD IN BUTTER & SUGAR.

COOK & STIR FOR 15 MINS. OR UNTIL OATMEAL TURNS INTO A PUDDING LIKE SUBSTANCE.

TAKE 10 COOKIES OUT OF BAG & CRUSH THEM INTO A FINE POWDER.

PUT IN THE BOTTOM OF A 10 LEVEL BOWL.

SLICE BANANAS INTO THIN PIECES.

PLACE SOME OF THEM OVER COOKIE CRUMBS IN THE BOWL, COVERING ALL THE CRUMBS.

FOLLOW UP WITH POURING A THIN LAYER OF THE OATMEAL OVER THE BANANAS.

THEN PLACE WHOLE COOKIES DOWN OVER OATMEAL RIGHT NEXT TO EACH OTHER, COMPLETELY COVERING THE OATMEAL.

REPEAT UNTIL YOUR BOWL IS FULL.

LET PUDDING SIT FOR AT LEAST 2 HOURS IN A COOL PLACE OR ROOM TEMPERATURE.

" TASTE GREAT TOPPED OFF WITH WHIPPED CREAM!"

SERVING SIZE: 5

PEANUT BUTTER CHOCOLATE BARS

(2) 16 OZ. BAG OF VANILLA WAFERS

(1) 14 OZ. PEANUT BUTTER SANDWICH COOKIES

(1) 9 OZ. BAG OF HOT COCOA

1 /2 CUP OF HONEY

(1) 18 OZ. JAR OF MELTED PEANUT BUTTER

1/2 OF CRUSHED PEANUTS

CRUSH ALL COOKIES & PLACE IN LARGE PROJECT BOX.

SPRINKLE A LITTLE WATER OVER ALL THE COOKIES.

ADD PEANUT BUTTER (LEAVE SOME FOR CHOCOLATE TOPPING) & HONEY TO A LARGE BOWL & MELT IN THE MICROWAVE.

POUR IN WITH CRUSHED COOKIES & MIX TOGETHER WITH HANDS. BUT FIRST LET IT COOL DOWN A LITTLE. WEAR PLASTIC GLOVES.

ONCE EVERYTHING IS MIXED REALLY WELL, BEGIN TO PRESS DOWN FIRMLY. MAKE SURE THAT THE BARS ARE EVEN ALL THE WAY AROUND.

POUR COCOA MIX IN A BOWL WITH A LITTLE PEANUT BUTTER THAT'S LEFT OVER & A LITTLE WATER. MIX WELL & SPREAD OVER BARS.

TOP OFF WITH CRUSHED PEANUTS. LET BARS SIT FOR AT LEAST 1 HOUR.

" SLICE IN SQUARES & IT'S PARTY TIME. ENJOY!!!"

SERVING SIZE: 10

TRIPLE CHOCOLATE CAKE W/ CHOCOLATE CREAM CHEESE FROSTING

(2) 16 OZ. BAGS OF VANILLA WAFERS

(2) 9 OZ. BAGS OF HOT COCOA

(5) 2 OZ. PKGS. OF CREAM CHEESE

4 PKGS. OF CHOPPED 'REESE'S PEANUT BUTTER CUP'

(1) 20 OZ. COKE SODA

1/4 CUP OF CRUSHED PEANUTS

CRUSH COOKIES & POUR 1 BAG IN 10 LEVEL MICROWAVABLE BOWL.

DO THE SAME FOR THE SECOND BAG IN A SEPARATE 10 LEVEL BOWL.

POUR IN 1/2 OF BAG HOT COCOA MIX IN ONE BOWL & THE OTHER 1/2 IN THE OTHER BOWL.

MIX & ADD SODA, 1/2 & 1/2. STIR INTO CAKE BATTER.

COOK EACH UNTIL IT RISES. CAREFUL NOT TO OVER-COOK.

USE A BUTTER KNIFE BY STICKING IT IN THE MIDDLE OF THE CAKE. IF IT COMES OUT CLEAN, THEN THE CAKE IS DONE. LET IT SIT FOR AT LEAST 15 MINS.

POUR THE OTHER BAG OF COCOA IN LARGE BOWL. ADD IN CREAM CHEESE & MIX INTO A FROSTING. ADD A LITTLE WATER IF IT'S TO THICK.

THEN ON A FLAT SURFACE, DUMP ONE OF THE CAKES OUT REALLY FAST, TIPPING THE BOTTOM OF THE BOWL. SPREAD A THIN LAYER OF FROSTING ON TOP.

DUMP SECOND CAKE ON TOP OF THE FIRST CAKE. SPREAD FROSTING OVER THE ENTIRE CAKE.

ADD REESE'S CUPS & PEANUTS. DECORATE IN WHICH EVER WAY YOU DESIRE.

" GREAT FOR BIRTHDAYS &/OR ANY OTHER SPECIAL OCCASIONS!!!"

SERVING SIZE: 10

*(BONUS) BIG RAJ'S HOMEMADE SAUCES

DIPPING SAUCES

MMMmmm BOY SAUCE (EXTENDED ADDITION)

1 CUP OF BBQ SAUCE

1 CUP OF CHUNKY PEANUT BUTTER

1/4 OF HONEY

3 TABLESPOONS OF THOUSAND ISLAND DRESSING

3 TABLESPOONS OF FRENCH DRESSING

2 TABLESPOONS OF MUSTARD

1/4 CUP OF CRUSHED RED PEPPERS

3 TABLESPOONS OF HOT SAUCE

3 TABLESPOONS OF KETCHUP

1 TABLESPOON OF SOY SAUCE

2 TABLESPOONS OF ONION POWDER

2 TABLESPOONS OF GARLIC POWDER

1 TABLESPOON OF SEASONING SALT

1/4 OF WATER

MIX TOGETHER WELL.

TARTAR SAUCE

 CUPS OF MAYO

1/2 CUP OF DICED DILL PICKLE

2 TABLESPOONS OF LEMON JUICE

HONEY MUSTARD SAUCE

2 CUP OF MAYO

2 TABLESPOONS OF CRUSHED RED PEPPERS

1 CUP OF MUSTARD

2 TABLESPOON OF DIJON MUSTARD

1/2 CUP OF HONEY